Contents

Preface

There are certain basic principles which we, as practising teachers, have come to value. This book has been written in the hope that it will help Key Stage 2 teachers who share those beliefs, to implement them in their own practice.

The book gives a variety of ideas and is intended for both the specialist and non-specialist. There are a number of ways teachers may use the ideas. Firstly, the teacher may use a single unit for a single lesson. Secondly, each unit has the potential to be developed in greater depth to form the basis of a series of lessons. Finally, the book can provide a number of starting points which teachers may take forward in their own ways.

Each theme contains 5 units and each unit has a structure consisting of:

- Exploring the ideas.
- Making the dance.
- Sharing the work.
- Possible developments.

A variety of teaching and learning styles have been used to enable both teacher and pupils to be fully involved, such as one in which the lesson is largely teacher directed to others in which pupils are given the initial stimulus and are asked to develop it as they choose. We have done this in the hope that readers will share the view that dance teaching requires more than making decisions about the topic of the lesson. Equally important are the teaching and learning strategies employed so that the pupils are fully involved in the work, and learn skills that will serve them both in and beyond the dance context.

The drawings are taken from work done by the authors with young people on the particular unit to which they refer. They are included to illustrate for teachers some of the many ways in which the tasks could be interpreted. A glossary has been included to clarify some of the terms in the book.

We hope that the book will offer some different approaches for teachers and generate some new ideas for the future.

Anne Allen and Janis Coley
Surrey
December 1994

David Fulton Publishers Ltd
London
Published in association with the Roehampton Institute

David Fulton Publishers Ltd
2 Barbon Close, London WC1N 3JX

First published in Great Britain by
David Fulton Publishers 1995

British Library Cataloguing in Publication Data

A catalogue record for this book is available from the British Library.

ISBN 1 – 85346 – 370 – 1

Typeset by RP Typesetters Ltd, 21 Wren Street, London WC1X 0HF
Printed in Great Britain by Bell & Bain Ltd, Glasgow

The Value of Dance in Education

The subject is essential for the personal development of each individual because it is the only one in which the mind, body and senses are fully integrated and share equal roles. Dance has always been used to express people's views of the world. As an accepted aim of education is the transmission of what is valued in the culture, the worth of dance in our society needs to be considered. It can be spontaneous and social, and every generation re-makes its own dance style.

We believe:

● Dance contributes to the pupil's personal growth, developing the mind, body and senses in a unique combination.

● All pupils have a right to a dance education, where the content and the ways of teaching are appropriate to their needs.

● Children should feel that the work is their own, and have the freedom to experiment within the structured environment of the dance lesson.

● Learning about dance consists of learning to make dances, perform and appreciate them.

Movement is our first language because it can express our thoughts and feelings, making it an important way of communicating. From the first movements of a new-born child to the intricacies of non-verbal communication, movement is a part of all us. It is also the vehicle for dance as a complex art-form.

Through our experiences, interacting with our surroundings, we acquire a 'cultural rucksack' which also influences our art. This in turn affects others we interact with. Education in dance aims to develop the skills, sensitivity and perception through which this continuous transaction takes place.

Physical skill, both fine and gross, control and co-ordination, flexibility, stamina and strength, are important to dance. Additionally, dancers learn to develop their sixth sense, the kinaesthetic, by increasing their awareness of what the body is doing, where and how it is moving. All learning initially takes place through the senses: the baby explores its immediate world through touch, taste etc. Through sensory perceptions, the body is the point of reference for our interaction with our environment. The dancer 'makes sense' of what is happening through the kinaesthetic, tactile, visual and auditory messages received.

As feelings are registered through the senses, so education of the senses will result in a greater awareness of the ways in which movement can be expressive. The development of this ability is crucial to children's artistic and aesthetic education, whether in the role of choreographer, performer or observer.

Just as the senses and feelings function in an integrated way with the body, the mind is also interdependent. For example, the understanding of concepts and the ability to recall are central to learning and also allow the dancer to visualise, reflect, interpret, imagine and create.

In addition to what is learned through the mind and body, children also learn to work with others. The dance lesson requires pupils to share the working space and at times to work with others in making and performing dances. Another kind of social interaction happens as we learn about different dance forms. This can help us to appreciate the contexts of the dance including the people who have initiated and developed them. Understanding the origins of the dance culture will enrich the child's experience and therefore contribute to the learning process.

The importance of dance in education is therefore multi-faceted. Its richness lies not only in how it develops the individual, but in the ways it can also contribute to children's social and cultural education.

Learning in Dance

For pupils, the dance lesson is primarily experiential. However learning in dance is more than only taking part in a physical activity. The opportunity to create their own dances is important for children and also learning to observe and reflect on their own work and that of others. Young people should be given the chance to develop the skills of choreographing, performing and appreciating. This three-stranded approach is an established model for teaching dance and has been used throughout this book. It is also present in the National Curriculum, through the statutory Attainment Target.

The three strands may be taught simultaneously; for example, pupils from an early age can make critical comments about dances as well as being able to make dances and perform them. Additionally, each strand makes certain demands on children.

Choreographing is the process of putting together movements with the ultimate aim of producing whole dances. On a basic level it involves making choices about movements. From the simplest decisions children make about their own actions, for example whether to jump on one or two feet, to pupils developing a group dance for performance, the demands remain essentially the same. Fundamental decisions must be made about such things as the actions and movement qualities to use and, perhaps more complexly, where and when the dancers will move in relation to each other and to the performance space. Children are learning how to create a unified whole appropriate to the stimulus they have been given.

The role of the teacher is to help pupils to develop a number of skills such as experimenting with ideas, analysing them and selecting the most suitable. It is important to allow time for pupils to work through these stages and for them to use their imagination in seeking innovative solutions to the task.

The interpersonal skills are equally important. Often in lessons, pupils will be working with others to make dances. Young people need to learn the skills of listening, negotiating and perhaps compromising before decisions are reached. On other occasions, one person may be given responsibility for all or part of the decision-making and it will be dependent on others to co-operate.

The performance strand may consist of pupils presenting dance choreographed by others or their own compositions. It could be to realise their planning in practice or setting out to present to a specific audience, albeit fellow class members. Performance skills include the basic actions of jumping, turning, balancing, taking and giving weight, and movement qualities such as the flow of energy and changes of speed. The teacher needs to provide challenges for pupils to improve the quality of their movements as they dance the way they control their movement and an awareness of the dance space itself. Learning the skills of presentation such as expression, clarity, projection and commitment must also be practised. Mastering these skills can improve self-image and increase confidence as the pupils become more competent, through encouragement and frequent opportunities, to present their work to others.

The third strand of appreciating requires the development of judgement and the ability to interpret dance, and it is possibly the most important strand as it permeates through the other two. Skilled dancers will constantly reflect on their work as they perform and adapt it accordingly. It is this ability which enables dancers to improve their performance by making it more accurate, more fluent and more manageable. It may also allow the creator to perceive the work as the audience might see it. Above all, this strand aims to foster an appreciation of quality by the pupil.

The first stage in the implementation of this strand is the development of observation skills, when children learn to look at specific aspects of a dance. This may be their own dance, other class members' work or movements shown by the teacher or on video. A simple viewing task, such as noticing and identifying one class member who has involved the whole body in the movement, is a start in helping pupils focus their attention on particular points which make good performance. The next stage is to learn to describe what is seen, for example, through comments such as, 'Those dancers are swinging their arms as they jump.' Later, comparisons can be made and pupils asked, 'Which dancer is making the widest shape?' Through these observational practices pupils will gain a sense of what are considered to be good points and will support the stage of making independent value judgements and explaining these by giving examples from their own perceptions. As pupils become more expert in the skill of appreciating, so they will be able to distinguish between a variety of dance forms as well as different levels of performance.

It is important that pupils feel free to make their own decisions and are not hampered by anticipating what the teacher expects them to say. If the climate of the lesson is supportive, that is if pupils feel free to speak, knowing that their views will be heard and respected, then they will gain confidence in their own judgements and this in turn will support their efforts at being creative. Evaluating dance is not a simple or passive process of observation and in the last resort, pupils will place an interpretation on the dance as a result of their own experience and perceptions. Such full and active involvement in the lesson is an important factor in developing pupils' capacity to evaluate in dance.

Glossary

The glossary offers an explanation of some of the terms used in the book as we explain **WHAT** dance actions are, **HOW** the body moves, **WHERE** the dancers moves to, the **RELATIONSHIPS** which have to be considered and **WHY** this particular dance is being made.

WHAT

●*PARTS OF THE BODY* – The body can be moved as a whole or certain parts can be emphasised.
Example: the elbow leads the action.

●*BODY DESIGN* – The way the dancer chooses to shape the body in movement or stillness.
Examples: angular, extended, wide, twisted, symmetrical.

●*TRAVEL* – Moving into another part of the space of any part(s) of the body.
Examples: walk, run, roll, crawl, slide.

●*GESTURE* – Actions where part or all of the body bends, stretches or twists, without travelling.
Examples: reach, contract, coil, rise, fall, open, close.

●*STILLNESS* – The body is actively held still.
Examples: freeze, pause, hesitate, halt.

●*JUMP* – The whole body takes off from and returns to the floor.
Examples: hop, spring, leap, bounce and variations.

●*TURN* – Actions which cause the whole body to face a different direction.
Examples: spin, spiral, whirl, wind.

Combinations of these actions – for example, gesturing whilst jumping and any variations – form the fabric of dance.

HOW

How the body moves will begin to give the movement particular qualities, sometimes referred to as 'dynamics'. The quality is what makes the movement expressive.

●*TIME* – Pace, changes of speed, rhythm and phrasing.
Examples: lingering, dashing, sauntering, slowing, accelerating, regular.

●*ENERGY* – Different degrees of body tension or power.
Examples: floppy, forceful, strong, heavy, relaxed, light.

●*FLOW* – Whether the action is performed freely and continuously or in a more hesistant, contained way.

WHERE

All the ways in which the dancer uses the space.

●*LEVELS.*
Examples: high, low, in the middle space.

●*DIRECTIONS.*
Examples: forwards, backwards, sideways.

●*PATHWAYS* – These can be on the floor or the pathways which the movement traces in the air.
Examples: travelling along zig-zag, tracing a circle in the air.

RELATIONSHIP

The relationship may be between parts of the body, the dancer and an object or one or more dancers.

●Relationships with the partner(s) will be established by factors such as how they orientate and how close they are to each other, with or without contact.
Examples: near to/far from, facing, back to back, above and below, matching and contrasting.

WHY

The dance will be shaped by the dancer's intentions. How (s)he moves will be influenced by the attitude and what the dance is about, which may be to communicate an idea, or purely for the sensation of enjoying moving in space.

Theme 1 **Visual Stimuli**

1.1 Dance Photos

Pupils should have as much chance to become familiar with professional dance works as possible. Two of these units introduce them to dance in this way and the concepts of gender role, costume, style, settings, etc.

Resources

Enough photos or copies for pupils to have easy access whilst working. These can be taken from books, programmes, dance magazines, newspapers etc.

Although music may be used to accompany the dance, it can inhibit the range of movements chosen.

Exploring the ideas

☐ Look at copies of one dance photo and discuss its features.

Teaching points
(a) As the aim is to encourage pupils' interest and observation skills, allow open-ended discussion first, before bringing in limitations.

(b) Then ask questions such as where is the weight being taken? Where is the focus? Is there contact or spaces between different parts of the body?

② Practise to achieve the same position as shown in the photo, constantly referring back to the resource picture.

Teaching points
(a) Physical limitations such as lack of flexibility of strength in balance may make accuracy difficult to achieve. Pupils may therefore have to modify the position.

(b) An alternative is to perform the position in a different plane, e.g. an upright position could be done on a horizontal plane.

Starting from photos

2

3 Explore different ways of moving into and out of the given design, e.g. turning into it.

Teaching point
Encourage a variety of responses, rather than a simple functional solution.

4 Choose a second, contrasting picture (possibly of a pair in contact) and repeat the process, including discussion, time permitting.

Possible developments

◇ Three photos can be introduced and a choice given in the order of use.

◇ Photos of off-balance or in flight designs can be used.

The teacher's own notes

Making the dance

Taking one photo as the starting position and one as the end, construct and perfect a short dance phrase, drawing on the possibilities planned previously.

Teaching points
(a) Pupils should be urged to try out as many ideas as possible, and only then, select, refine and practise their chosen one.

(b) If a pair photo has been chosen, time must be allowed for pupils to plan jointly how their individual dance phrases will interact.

Sharing the work

All solos or duos are demonstrated, one-third of the class at a time, group A to perform first.

Teaching points
(a) Observers should be divided into two groups. Group B looks for and comments on accuracy in the body designs, reproduced from the photos. Group C looks for and comments on the originality of the linking sections.

(b) Groups rotate, which means that each group has a chance to perform and to observe against the different criteria each time.

1.2 Spatial Design

This visual design elements of objects such as visual art works, sculpture or found items – i.e. line, shape, balance, symmetry or otherwise – are explored. These are translated into aspects of the dance, such as body design, floor and air pathways.

Resources

1. Pictures (non-figurative) including those of three-dimensional objects.

2. Objects such as pieces of wood, rope, shells, cones, crystals, rock or appropriate man-made ones.

Exploring the ideas

Pupils are given either pictures *or* objects.

1 Identify a shape contained within this which you notice and then explore ways of translating this into still body designs, e.g. triangle, spiral.

Teaching point
Using the three planes will give variety to the ideas, i.e. circular pathways using the up/down, forward/back, sideways dimensions.

2 Trace the chosen design as a pathway on the floor.

Teaching point
Encourage changes of levels, travelling ideas, directions etc. For some pupils it may be possible to take these from the original stimulus.

3 Develop the design as an air pattern, using a variety of body parts.

Teaching point
Again, change of size, level and plane will be valuable.

Making the dance

Find ways of using your three interpretations of the design – i.e. as still shapes, floor and air patterns – and combine them to create the dance.

Teaching point
The three ideas can be used consecutively or simultaneously, which would be a more advanced interpretation.

Sharing the work

Show the original object to a partner and point out which aspects of the design you chose. Then perform your dance.

Teaching point
Partners observe for and comment on the imaginative interpretation of the task.

The teacher then selects a few of the pieces to be demonstrated to the class.

Designing with the body

Possible developments

◇ Choose two contrasting elements from the design and perform them simultaneously, i.e. curving body shape and angular air patterns.

◇ Link with a partner who is working from a very different design, find ways of combining your dance phrases into a duo.

The teacher's own notes

1.3 Every Picture Tells A Story

Resources

1. Enough pictures containing people for the class to have one each.

2. Pupils can help themselves to phrase their movements by 'playing' a piece of music in their minds which would be appropriate for that character.

Exploring the ideas

Each pupil is given a picture or photograph containing one or more people.

☐ Think who the person might be.

Teaching point
The character will begin to emerge through questions such as: What is the person's age? What are they wearing? How do they feel in these clothes? Name? Where do they come from? How do they feel about life? There are no 'right' answers, pupils are free to interpret.

Some of you will be selected to feed back your ideas. If any pupil is devoid of ideas, the class can be invited to help with suggestions.

☐ Working with a chair, adopt a sitting position which you think is appropriate for this character.

Teaching point
Encourage attention to detail especially whether the lower body is being used. Where are the feet placed? What is the person's posture? Where is the focus? Why are they sitting there?

☐ Find a gesture that fits in with the character.

Teaching points
(a) This may be with an isolated part of the body, i.e. a turn of the head, crossing the feet, etc., or could involve a shift of weight of the whole body, e.g. to lean forward, stand up etc.

(b) Are the speed/energy dynamics appropriate to the character?

☐ This time, repeat the gesture in such a way that it takes you away from the chair.

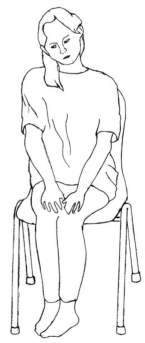

Creating a character

Teaching point
The dancers should consider:

- *In what ways are the dynamics being used?*
- *Is the body position still in character?*
- *Does the focus change?*

Making the dance

Construct a dance around the character by starting with your sitting position on the chair. Make your first gesture, repeat the gesture so that it takes you away from the chair and then complete the dance by returning to the chair in any way you like to finish in your original seated position.

Teaching points
(a) Encourage pupils to stay in character throughout.
(b) The sitting position must be repeated as accurately as possible, since this encourages movement memory.

Sharing the work

Solos are performed, several at a time.

Teaching point
Observers look for and comment on clear realisation of character through the dance phrase.

Possible developments

◇ Within the given character, find different ways of being in contact with the chair, perhaps placing the chair in unconventional positions.

◇ Invent your own character and explore the same task.

◇ With one or more partners, explore through movement, possible interactions between the characters.

1.4 Moving Objects

Here the qualities within the movement itself or different materials such as kinetic executive toys, water and kites are used to determine the features of the dance.

Resources

1. Objects which show movement, as wide a range as possible. Pupils may contribute their own.

2. A chart for recording pupils' observations.

Choice of music will depend on the objects used.

Exploring the ideas

The intention here is to consider movement, through studying the dynamics rather than spatial patterns, as in some other units. The possible range of objects is endless, but they should be chosen with the age-group in mind in order to stimulate interest.

Pupils watch the movement of an object (examples: clock mechanism, executive toy, parachute, timers which used coloured gels and water) and describe in as many ways as possible **how** it moves, including metaphor, e.g. spiralling like a snake.

The teacher selects out the words suggested by the pupils that refer to the dynamics of speech or power and records them on a chart.

Move into a space and sit down to experiment with ways of re-creating the **qualities** of the movement, using hands only. Once this is achieved, use the arms, then shoulders and upper body. Move onto

the feet and keeping the same qualities, use the movements to travel.

Teaching point
The aim of introducing this through using the hands only is to achieve the best quality of movement through using the parts of the body which we have most control over. Secondly, focusing on the hands initially will eliminate the idea that pupils are expected to 'act out' the object, which is in fact merely provided as a stimulus.

Moving like gel

8

Making the dance

① Be aware of how you change the speed, i.e. the way the movement begins and ends, either abruptly or gradually, since this will help your timing and phrasing. Additionally the energy level may also change in a way which can be observed. Now incorporate this into your movement phrase, by establishing the beginning and ending. For example, the impulse with which a parachute is launched and slow loss of power as it eventually comes to rest.

② Repeat the movement phrase, two or three times, depending on length, concentrating on the transition in dynamics, build-up of momentum.

Teaching points
(a) The speed/energy/flow factors are the focus of this work, pupils should show clearly how these change and develop during the performance.
(b) Pupils will need to establish how to link the repetitions.

Sharing the work

Pupils demonstrate in half-class groups.

Teaching point:
Observers comment on how well the quality of the original object has been re-created.

Possible developments

◇① Two or more objects offering contrasting qualities. Pupils use both and combine the dance phrases.

◇② A variety of objects is offered, pupils are free to choose.

1.5 Videos

A further opportunity to introduce pupils to recognised dance works arises when they study these as video. The range of possibilities for enriching their own work will depend on their age and experience, but could include learning set studies, analysing style and extracting movement motifs.

Resources

1. Any published videos of recognised dance works.

2. Videos recorded from television broadcast, including pop vidoes, may be used within the constraints of the licensing laws.

Dance is essentially about movement and therefore video is an important resource which is often under-used. The range of possible uses is considerable. In this unit, pupils are asked to consider aspects which will allow them to explore the style of the dance.

Exploring the ideas

Pupils should be given general background information about the dance work, i.e the title of the work, the names of the performer(s), company and choreographer, what the dance is about and the context of the extract.

1 Watch the extract several times and identify the movements which catch your attention or seem important.

Teaching points
(a) The extract chosen should be brief, depending on pupils' experience, but initially no longer than 2 to 3 minutes.

(b) The criteria for viewing need to be set first, so that pupils know what to give their attention to.

(c) Comments should be invited between each viewing.

2 Try out and practise one or more movements you have seen, with the chance to return and watch the video again as and when necessary.

Teaching points
(a) This provides a good opportunity for pupils to assist each others' learning.

(b) It is important to recognise that pupils with the best powers of observation may not be those who are technically the most competent. Their strengths should be acknowledged.

3 Repeat the process, as often as time permits, taking a different movement or phrase.

Learning dance from video

Teaching point
Some pupils will prefer to concentrate on and perfect a single movement or phrase. All pupils should be limited to the number of movements or phrases that they can retain and perform without loss of quality.

Making the dance

You will be given the option of *either* using the material to create a dance of your own *or* to reproduce a single movement or phrase from the video as accurately as possible.

Teaching point
This choice should be offered on condition that given an appropriately challenging video, pupils have extended their own vocabularly in the experimental work, i.e. are using movements with which they are unfamiliar.

Sharing the work

Pupils are grouped according to whether they have learnt part of the dance or chosen to develop it.

Teaching point
Pupils should be acknowledged for their ability to re-create the movements accurately, within the style of the piece. Those choosing the other option should be acknowledged for their imaginative recreation.

Possible developments

◇ Pupils can learn set studies from appropriate vidoes, either taught by the teacher or directly from the video.

◇ Pupils may work on the formations, i.e. the position of one dancer in relation to other(s), without also being tied to performing accurately the dance movements.

The teacher's own notes

Theme 2 Games

2.1 Olympic Games

Pupils have the chance to choose their own sport and base their dance on warm-up activities and actions relevant to that sport.

Resources

1. Videos of sporting/and or Olympic events.

2. The opening sections of *Troy Games* choreographed by Robert North.

3. Music: Themes from TV sports programmes, e.g. *Grandstand.*

Exploring the ideas

1 Discuss the different events which make up the Olympic Games. Can any pupils describe or demonstrate characteristic movements which would identify the sport, i.e. speed skating, weight lifting?

2 Choose a sport which has an interesting and characteristic action to it. Think about the three stages of preparation, action and recovery. How do you prepare for the action? How does the movement follow through? Try variations on performing the movement: can you travel as you do it?

Teaching points
(a) Particular praise should be given to unusual choices of sports.

(b) Use the image of throwing a ball: can pupils tell you where the speed and energy increase? Decrease? Can they put the same climax effect into their action?

3 Repeat your action three times, the first one realistically, then each time making the action larger by adding turning, jumping, and/or travelling, e.g. the discus thrower, swings, travels and turns to launch the discus.

4 *The warm-up* – Which parts of the body does your sport particularly use? Find two or three different movements which will loosen those joints and repeat it as a pattern, as if warming up for your event.

Teaching point
Encourage pupils to work the joints to their full range, and in different planes.

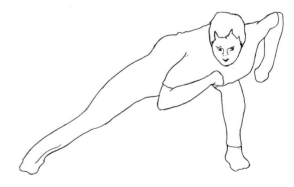

Speed skating

Making the dance

① *The warm-up* – Taking your loosening up ideas, make a pattern to last 32 (or 64) beats.

Teaching points
(a) Encourage variety and involvement of whole body, focusing attention on the specific part.
(b) Encourage a concentrated and purposeful way of working here.

② *The main event* – Move immediately into the starting position for your sports action and carry it out three times, holding the finishing position until everyone has completed.

Sharing the work

Demonstrate your work to the class.

Teaching point
Comments are asked for on pupils whose sport can be clearly identified and those who have succeeded in exaggerating the action each time.

Possible developments

Group developments, such as marching patterns, flag-waving, etc., can be added.

The teacher's own notes

2.2 Snooker

Circular air and floor pathways together with body designs are explored through the theme. Partner ideas such as meeting, parting, action and reaction are also part of the dance.

Resources

1. Snooker balls or video of a game to demonstrate the rebound action.

2. Music: Various tracks from *The Entertainer* soundtrack. Shannachie SHAN 98015.

Exploring the ideas

☐ *The rebound:*

(i) In twos, stand facing, hands flat against your partner's, lean towards each other and push to spring away. Find different ways of doing this, by varying the parts of the body touching.

Teaching points
(a) The contact is co-operative, weight should be given and taken with control.

(b) Emphasise the pushing away – not just leaving the partner.

(c) Suggest that pupils try large and small body parts.

(d) Can they vary the directions in which they leave their partners?

(ii) Decide on one way of meeting and parting from your partner and then repeat as in (i) but this time approach your partner with a run first. Try two other ways of doing this.

Teaching points
(a) Words such as 'bounce', 'impact', 'cannon', 'ricochet', 'spin-off', 'collide', 'rebound' all performed with control and co-operation, may help the class to develop the image for this work.

(b) The running should be 'busy', e.g. upright stance, high knee lift, pumping arm action but with speed controlled.

(iii) Use all three of your meeting/parting ideas. Decide on pathways to be used to approach and leave your partner in order to meet again.

Teaching point
Encourage a variety of pathways, e.g. curved, spinning off.

Circular air pattern

2 *Spinning and rotating:*

Explore circular body actions, find different ways of turning and travelling, e.g. rolling, spinning, cart-wheeling.

Teaching points
(a) SAFETY: Pupils should be encouraged to rotate in different directions and around different axes, in order to keep their balance.

(b) Pupils should try to keep a rounded body shape during the action where possible, this will give original ways of performing the 'gymnastics' moves of a cart-wheel, roll etc.

(c) Encourage high and medium rounded body shapes too, even though they are initially more difficult.

Making the dance

The dance begins with individuals performing a combination of their ideas for spinning and rotating. Pupils must decide where they start, their pathway, and where they finish in the room.

From this point, pupils perform the rebound section of the dance, i.e. the meeting and parting section, already worked out with their partners.

After the third partner impact, the dance ends with individuals returning to their original place in the room, using their spinning and turning actions again.

Teaching points
(a) Timing is crucial and will depend on good observation of each other.

(b) Encourage humorous interpretations, especially in the running and impact sections.

Sharing the work

Half the class demonstrates in its pairs.

Teaching point:
Observation should be directed towards interesting partner interaction and good co-operation, i.e. timing.

Possible developments

◇ When pupils can turn, spin, etc. with control, increase of speed in the solo sections will add interest.

◇ The meeting and parting section can be developed for partners to go over or under each other with contact.

◇ A third section to represent the cue, a group line-up with a unison pushing or travelling action, maintaining a straight, thin shape, can be added.

The teacher's own notes

15

2.3 Cat's Cradle

The dance involves pupils working with large elastic loops to form changing patterns in a life-sized version of the cat's cradle.

Resources

1. Loops of elastic, between 1 and 1.5 metres in length, securely tied.

2. Group loops, between 2 and 4 metres in length, securely tied.

3. Parents' or grandparents' knowledge of hand cat's cradle designs.

Exploring the ideas

SAFETY NOTE: A soft type of elastic should be used, and pupils made aware that they must maintain their grip whilst working.

1 Experiment individually with the elastic loop, finding different ways of gripping it, with a variety of body parts, then stretching out to make as many shapes as possible.

Teaching points
(a) Encourage the use of as many different parts of the body to give variety, e.g. waist, back to knee, heel.

(b) Encourage awareness of two- and three-dimensional shapes, symmetrical and asymmetrical ones.

2 With one or more partners (depending on the teacher's estimate of co-operation skills), repeat the work from 1, working with the larger loops. Smooth transitions from one design to another should be the aim. You may experiment with moving over and under the elastic.

Teaching points
(a) Groups should be able to achieve larger, longer and more complex shapes.

(b) The design of the body is as important as the lines made by the elastic, encourage pupils to be aware of this.

Making the dance

Choose, plan and practise a series of movements and designs so that you can repeat them.

Using elastic to create spatial patterns

Teaching point
Once pupils are clear what they are doing, it may become possible to change the speed of the action, e.g. to spring suddenly into one of their group shapes, or to weave slowly into another.

Sharing the work

Demonstrate to one other group.

Teaching points
(a) Pupils should identify groups who work well together, i.e. who watch each other and adapt their movements.
(b) Interesting designs should also be noted.

Possible developments
Group size can be increased.

The teacher's own notes

2.4 A Pack of Cards

The dance is developed from the ideas of shuffling and fanning out.

Resources

1. Pack of cards.
2. Music: Scot Joplin rags.

Exploring the ideas

☐1 *Shuffling the pack* – In groups of four, start near each other and practise changing places in the formation, using different ways of dodging quickly in and out, e.g. with shuffling steps.

Teaching points
(a) Working in groups. It may help every pupil to contribute, if a different leader is appointed for the two sections and it is established that all pupils' ideas are explored before decisions are made. Pupils who are still could maintain the same flat, two-dimensional body shape, which will help the moving partner.
(b) Suggest that dancers try starting and finishing other than in standing positions, e.g. lying down.

☐2 *Fanning out the cards* – In the same groups, find a close, compact group shape and explore ways of reaching out, making curves pathways and group designs to create the fan shape and coming back into the compact formation.

Teaching points
(a) In order to contrast with the first section, this part could be performed slowly.
(b) Individuals may move out one at a time (canon) or together (unison).

Making the dance

In your groups, begin with your shuffling dance and then change to the fanning out section, finishing with an open fan design.

Teaching point
Encourage the contrast of speed between the shuffling and fanning sections.

Sharing the work

Several 'packs' perform at once.

Teaching points
(a) Pupils should look for close co-operation within the group.
(b) Interesting or unusual group fan designs should be noted.

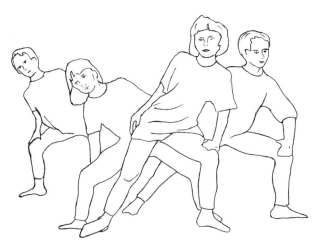

Fan formation

Possible developments

◇ Toppling the pack. The 'domino effect' could be explored with pupils beginning in a line, and falling (with control!) in turn. This could be added as a third section.

◇ Different characters could be developed, e.g. Knave (impish, mischief maker), Kings and Queens (stately, possible introduction of court style dance), Ace (powerful).

The teacher's own notes

2.5 Chinese Chequers

The design of the board, based on triangles and the way in which the pieces move over each other, is used as the elements for the dance.

Resources

1. Chinese Chequers boards.
2. Music: Various tracks from *Musique Traditionelle de Chine*. Festival 114934.

Exploring the ideas

1 *Zig-zag travelling patterns:*

(i) Explore running along zig-zag pathways, jumping to give clear changes of direction. Vary the jumps, by taking off from and landing on one or two feet.

Teaching point
There are five basic jumps which can be explored. It may help to give them names, if the class is not familiar with them:

2→ 2 feet = bounce.

1→same = hop.

1→ other = leap.

1→ 2 = hopscotch (first part)

2→ hopscotch (second part).

(ii) Using the jumps travel along a zig-zag pathway, keeping the changes of direction clear. Try sideways or backwards jumps as well as forward ones.

Teaching points
(a) Accuracy in the floor patterns, variety in the jumps will give quality to the work.

(b) If the children are unfamiliar with the five basic jumps, it may be necessary to introduce just one or two as variations.

2 Find still shapes that you can hold, where the body is making one or more triangles. Experiment with low and high shapes, upright and flat ones.

3 Find ways of supporting the body on three points, so that your design has a triangular base. Repeat the same base, but find a different body shape which you can make above it.

Teaching point
Time permitting, pupils can combine 2 *and* 3 *, i.e. the body design and the base are both triangular.*

4 Trio work. Two of the group hold their shapes whilst the third experiments with ways of travelling over and under. Select the most appropriate shapes, which will help your partners to develop interesting ways of travelling.

Triangular body shapes

Teaching point
Shapes need to be held with good body tension and still. Travelling must be done carefully.

Making the dance

① Choose a place in the room to meet your partners. Work out your zig-zag pathways to arrive in a triangular formation and at the same time if possible.

Teaching point
Change of pace, or pausing may be necessary to accommodate partners.

② You will each be given a letter in your group A, B and C. B and C hold their triangular positions whilst A crosses over and under them in turn. As soon as B has been crossed s/he follows, crossing C and then A who has returned to the start and taken up position; C follows as soon as B has passed. The dance finishes with all three in individual triangular designs.

Teaching point
Children will need to plan the links between their designs and travelling patterns to achieve fluency. Watching each other carefully will also be essential.

Sharing the work

Each trio performs to another. Observers give positive feedback, before changing over.

Teaching point
Observers look for clear zig-zag pathways and good ideas for still positions.

Teacher selects one or two of the best pieces of group work selected on these criteria, to be performed to the whole class.

Possible developments

◇ Pupils may use contact when crossing their partners.

◇ Jumps may be varied by aiming for height or length.

◇ Braids may be used to identify groups in the class, e.g. red, blue green. Each 'team' could begin in a triangular formation, before breaking into the zig-zag travelling patterns to meet partners from the other two colour teams.

◇ Trios could finish in a joint triangular design, with or without contact, variation of level, etc.

The teacher's own notes

Theme 3 Non-Verbal Communication

3.1 My Name is . . .

The dance is developed from the ideas of writing the name and uses a variety of parts of the body to lead the action, changes of direction and size as well as stillness and movement.

Resources

Music: 'Clog Dance' from *La Fille Mal Gardee*. Ballet Spectacular. RPO Pickwick ZCRP 07010. 'March of the Meanies'. *Yellow Submarine* soundtrack. Parlophone EMI TOPCS 7070.

Exploring the ideas

1 Trace your first name, one letter at a time in the air in front of you.

2 Enlarge the writing, so that it fills the whole room.

Teaching point
Pupils should try to go as high and low as possible.

3 Now write your name with your back, still keeping the letters large.

4 Choose another part of the body and write your name as small as possible.

Teaching point
Look for pupils who are making the letters accurate and precise.

5 Lie down and choose any part of the body other than the hand, write your name on the ceiling.

6 Choose any part of the body, write your name again, but this time change the way you are facing during it.

Tracing pathways in the air

22

Teaching point
Throughout, encourage pupils to involve the whole body in the writing action.

7 Can you shape your body into any of the letters of your name?

Teaching point
Ask pupils to be as accurate as possible and to use the whole body.

Making the dance

Using a variety of body parts, combine the ideas of body shape and pathways in the air, make a dance that represents the letters in your name.

Teaching points
(a) Remind the class to use both large and small actions, also travelling and the whole body.
(b) Pupils should be challenged to make it as original as possible!

Sharing the work

Pupils demonstrate in groups.

Teaching point
Observers look for unusual ways of interpreting the task.

Possible developments

Choreograph a dance with a partner, finding ways (including making contact), of combining names.

The teacher's own notes

3.2 Meeting and Greeting

Non-verbal communication is said to make up over 90% of human interaction. The next two units explore the ways in which recognised gestures are used to give messages.
The first of these units takes the dance idea from ways of greeting.

Resources

Music: 'Lovely Day'. *Greatest Hits: Bill Withers*. CBS 40 32343. 'Let's Hear it for the Boy'. *Footloose* soundtrack. CBS 4630004. 'Shake your Tail Feather'. *The Blues Brothers* soundtrack. Atlantic 450715.

Exploring the ideas

1 *Partner work:*

(i) In twos, experiment with different ways of shaking hands with each other, one hand, the other, both together. Try four handshakes with right, four with left, then two of each, then one right and one left, one right one left. This patterning introduces a way of phrasing the movements. Try ways of shaking hands without facing each other, e.g. back to back. Try adding a movement, such as a turn between each set of handshakes. Experiment with different grips, try above the head and between the feet.

Teaching point
Encourage pupils to work with the rhythm of the music.

(ii) Now try 'shaking hands' with different parts of the body, e.g. spine, make contact and 'shake' or link lower legs and shake.

(iii) Think of other gestures which can be used to represent greeting.

Teaching point
Examples may be waving, slapping hands.

2 Join with another pair and discuss ideas for greeting in fours.

Shaking hands

24

Making the dance

Section 1: Partner work

Using any of the ideas for shaking hands explored above, create a short section of the dance. Make sure that some of the ideas are repeated: this will give the section structure. Finish your partner near the other pair.

Teaching point
Pupils should use a range of contrasting possibilities.

Section 2: Group work

Select some of the ideas discussed in your foursome and form them into a second section of the dance.

Teaching point
The pair which finishes first, holds its final position until other partners are ready.

Sharing the work

Several fours perform at once.

Teaching point
Observers should look for and comment on good use of the rhythm and phrasing.

Possible developments

This dance could offer scope for another section choreographed by the teacher (can be derived from the children's ideas) on step patterns developed within the rhythm, this could introduce the dance and bring partners together or to link sections 1 and 2.

The teacher's own notes

3.3 Superstitions

This dance takes as its starting point gestures which accompany superstitious beliefs.

Resources

1. Dictionaries of superstitions.

2. Research amongst parents and grandparents, friends from different cultures.

3. Music: 'Boadicea'. Enya. BBC Cassettes ZCF 605.

Exploring the ideas

1 Discuss superstitions and the movements related to them, e.g. avoiding cracks in pavements, throwing salt over your shoulder, going round not under a ladder. Choose one and do it accurately. Repeat, being really aware of what you are doing. Try to repeat it exactly the same each time.

2 Repeat the action, enlarging it, possibly using another body part until the size of the action takes you to another area of the room. Try combining two or three variations.

Teaching point
If the phrase is very short, it can be performed twice.

3 Choose another superstition and its action and repeat the whole process so that you now have two different movement phrases.

Teaching point
Greater variety will result if children choose actions that are led by different body parts, i.e. touch wood, jump pavement cracks.

Making the dance

Using all or any of your ideas, combine the movements to form one short solo dance. Remember that you will need to invent an appropriate starting and an ending position. Make sure that your movements link together without loss of continuity.

Teaching point
Make pupils aware that repetition as well as contrasting movements can be used in their compositions.

Crossing fingers (variations)

Sharing the work

All solo dances are performed in turn.

Teaching points
(a) Groups may be arranged according to which superstitions were taken as starting points. This will demonstrate the variety of response.

(b) Observers should look for imaginative use of the original action.

Possible developments

1. The same approach but in groups.

2. The teacher selects the superstition and original actions on which the dance will be based.

3. Emphasise the contrasting use of dynamics, e.g. changes of speed and power or energy.

The teacher's own notes

3.4 The Message is in the Picture

A painting is used as the stimulus for this dance and the process is one of translating symbols into movements as well as exploring the pathways and directions which the picture suggests.

Resources

Picures by Kandinsky, Miro or Klee.

If only one copy is available, it may be necessary to use several alternative paintings which have similarities.

Abstract pictures will be the most suitable.

Exploring the ideas

1 Look at the picture and describe it.

Teaching point
Encourage pupils to identify shapes, colours, size and angles, rather than looking for meaning.

2 The teacher explains that the picture is going to be used as a script for their dance and that the features they have identified will be used as symbols to represent elements in the dance.

Decide which symbols you want to represent which actions, for example: travelling (includes jumping, turning); gesture (e.g. stretching, twisting); or holding a still position.

Teaching point
The choice can be made by consensus within the class, individually, or teacher directed if the class needs to work on one aspect in particular.

3 Explore the ideas contained within the picture, by choosing where to start in the picture and following your own 'route' and translating symbols into movement as you come to them.

Teaching points
(a) It may help pupils to imagine that the painting is transferred to the floor so that they can travel through it. This will also help pupils to remember their starting point and their route.

(b) Pupils may choose to use part of the painting only.

Translating symbols

Making the dance

Make sure that you have a clear beginning and end to your dance. Work on the ways in which one movement leads into the next, including travelling between symbols. Repeat, practise and memorise your dance.

Teaching points
(a) Pupils may choose to start with a shape from the picture.
(b) Encourage pupils to give as much attention to developing the travelling actions as to the symbols themselves.
(c) Be aware that your paths may cross others.

Sharing the work

Demonstrate your dance to a partner. Change over.

Teaching point
Partner is to see whether the dance is joined together without interruption. Discuss views with partner. These comments should be helpful and constructive.

Possible developments

◇ Instead of assigning **actions**, an alternative is to assign **dynamics** to the symbols. For example: sharp, swift, lingering, forceful or gentle. This will depend on how much experience and understanding the pupils have.

◇ Using different or more complex paintings.

The teacher's own notes

3.5 Dance Scripts

Recording dances is a way of helping movement memory and developing visual skills, and can be a creative source. This unit explores non-verbal methods of making scripts of dance.

Resources

1. Paper, coloured pens.

2. Codes from the Highway Code, map keys, music. Other languages such as hieroglyphics, Arabic, Chinese etc., may all give ideas.

3. Examples of recognised dance notation.

Exploring the ideas

[1] The teacher sets a short movement phrase from the words **dash – jump – unwind** and **reach.**

[2] Experiment with ways of doing each word. Choose one version for each.

Making the dance

Decide on the direction and pathways of each action, and then practise the dance, repeating it several times until you can make smooth transitions from one action to the next.

Teaching points
(a) Pupils may need to be reminded to be aware of others.

(b) Ask pupils to make it clear if their movements are fast or v-e-r-y s-l-o-w.

(c) Is there clear body design (body shape) in the stillness at beginning and end?

Sharing the work

① If you had to remember this dance for a very long time, what is it important to record?

Teaching point
Suggestions – actions, pathways, directions, speeds, body design.

② Now record your dance, without using words and if possible through signs rather than 'pin men'. More than one colour may be used.

Teaching point
A large square piece of paper rather than rectangular may encourage a freer approach.

③ Once the scripts are completed, the teacher selects interesting or original examples. The author explains the process to the class.

Reaching

Teaching point
Scripts which are free flow and follow the route of the dance rather than a series of lines as in writing, will be more helpful.

Scripts which record dynamics (speed and energy of the actions) will be more rare and should be noted.

Possible developments

◇ One pupil's script is given to a partner to interpret.

◇ If used regularly, simple symbols can be agreed, e.g. direction arrows.

The teacher's own notes

Theme 4 The Egyptians

4.1 The Frieze

The dance draws on the Egyptian figures represented on vases, wall paintings etc., and develops the idea into a human frieze.

Resources

1. Pictures, postcards of Egyptian figures, from works of art (British Museum).
2. Music: 'The Egyptian March'. Johann Strauss. *1993 New Year's Concert*. Philips 4384934PH. *Indo-Arabic Variations*. Baligh Hamdi and Majid Khan. Playasound 1989 PS 65035.

Making the dance

① Join in threes or fours and show each other your still positions. Decide how you can make three-group friezes from them.

Teaching point
The frieze may be in a line, on the diagonal. Individuals within the line may be sideways on, facing each other, etc.

Exploring the ideas

Study the comment on the characteristic ways in which the human figure is represented in Egyptian works of art, i.e. shoulders and torso square on, head and feet in profile, shoulders, elbows and wrists often held at angles. Try to remember and re-create the positions, then experiment with versions of your own. Choose three contrasting ones which you can perform well.

Teaching points
(a) Draw attention to the tension needed in twisting the body to maintain the designs accurately.

(b) Encourage pupils to choose or invent positions which use different levels for variety.

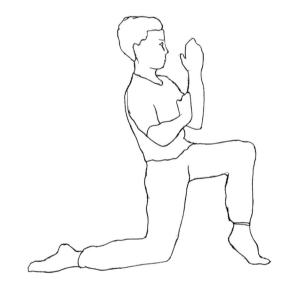

The frieze

② Find a way of moving from one frieze to another. Can you do this within the style of the frieze?

Teaching point
The still positions need to be held until everyone in the group has arrived at a stationary position. They may be in different positions within the frieze, for variety.

Sharing the work

Perform the work one or two groups at a time.

Teaching point
Observers should be asked to look for groups which manage to achieve and maintain the style of the original works of art.

Possible developments

Pupils may develop longer travelling patterns which build on the same characteristics as the still designs, which can then be used by the groups.

The teacher's own notes

4.2 Hieroglyphics

Hieroglyphics encapsulate objects or ideas in written language form. In this piece of work, pupils develop movement hieroglyphics (i.e. motifs) which represent aspects of Egyptian life.

Resources

1. Examples of hieroglyphics. Pictures of traditional fishing, hunting, farming methods.

2. Music: See music resources for Unit 4.1 (*The Frieze*, page 32).

Exploring the ideas

1 Discuss the way in which hieroglyphics are symbols which capture the essential meaning of the word. Develop single movements which similarly can represent fishing, farming or hunting, important activities in the lives of the ancient Egyptians.

Teaching points
(a) Pupils may need some explanation of methods, for example, sticks were thrown at birds in flight, fish were speared.

(b) Actions will fall into categories of moving outwards away from the body, e.g. scattering seed, whirling and throwing net – or gathering in, as in drawing in a net, harvesting etc.

2 Experiment with making the action change level as you perform it.

3 Extend the action by combining it with a turn, travelling or jump.

Making the dance

Alternate between the original version, on the spot, of your motif and extended one. Make sure that the beginning and end of the dance is made clear through still positions. In addition, you will need to plan how to link the two parts.

Teaching point
Make sure that pupils show clearly the difference between the motif and the development, without losing the whole-body involvement in the first.

Sharing the work

Whole class demonstrates to the teacher. The teacher selects the most original ideas to be performed for the class.

Trawling

*The teacher will need to explain the criteria
s/he has applied, i.e. use of whole-body,
unusual actions or use of directions and/or
dynamics.*

Possible developments

The whole class can be choreographed into
one by the teacher putting pupils into one
of three groups, which begin (and
therefore end) on a signal at different
times.

The teacher's own notes

4.3 The River Nile

The idea of the movement hieroglyphic is built upon. The class develops a range of ideas to represent the Nile and these are used to form the basis of a group dance. The piece gives children the advantages of learning a set study – developing their powers of observation and extending their movement vocabulary from ideas generated within the class.

Resources

1. Any video, poetry or still pictures of water moving, e.g. Leonardo da Vinci drawings.

2. Music: See music resources for Unit 4.1 (*The Frieze*, page 32).

Exploring the ideas

1. Explore the characteristics of moving water through a pupil brainstorm, e.g. flowing, winding, undulating, swirling, tidal. Discuss the fact that the Nile swells and floods.

2. Individually, make up a travelling motif to represent the flowing water, which uses your whole body.

Teaching point
Pupils should try to get the quality (i.e. continuous, flowing) whilst making the movements as large as possible.

3. The teacher chooses one, two or three pupils with successful ideas to perform and *either* select one *or* a combination of parts of their actions for the class to learn.

Teaching points
(a) Choose pupils who are using their spines, so that the body design (body shape) is rounded, arching or curving.

(b) It is important to choose an idea which the class can achieve, with practice.

Making the dance

① If chosen, demonstrate your movement, and the class will practise it until they have mastered it. The second and third parts are then added in the same way. Practise the new combination until you can perform it well. You may be asked to assist others with learning the part you have contributed. Now combine in twos and work at matching your timing. When you have achieved this, repeat the process in fours, until the whole group can perform in unison.

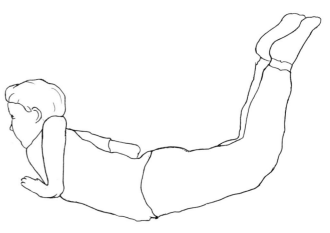

Undulating

② All line up in their fours, in one corner of the room facing the diagonal. One row of four begins and as they start the motif for the second time, the second row joins in and so on until the whole class has traversed the room.

Teaching point
To maximise the space, pupils must wait out of the way and be ready to make their entrance on cue.

Sharing the work

Half-class demonstrations.

Teaching point
Look for dancers who have captured the essence of the moving water motif, i.e. are moving in a flowing continuous way, using their spines.

Possible developments

The dance can end with the 'Nile flooding': once the first rwo reaches the far corner, and the class is spread across the diagonal, everyone sinks down to lying and slowly rolls outwards to the sides.

Teaching point
(a) The first row will need to initiate this as they cannot see the rest of the group.
(b) Check that spacing is adequate.

The teacher's own notes

4.4 In Search of the Ancient Tomb

An opportunity for children to re-enact, through dance, the experience of the modern-day discoveries of the tombs of the Pharaohs.

Resources

1. Accounts of the discovery of the tombs.

2. Pictures of artefacts, e.g. Tutankhamun's mask.

3. British Museum.

4. History resource books.

5. Music: 'Promenade'. *Pictures at an Exhibition*. Chandos ABTD 1466.

Exploring the ideas

☐ *The museum visit* – Discuss visits to museums or galleries. Stroll around as though viewing in a museum, pausing in still position to study the artefacts. Is the object near or far? Large or small?

Teaching point
Encourage realism, i.e. head to one side, hand supporting chin, etc.

☐ *Moving back in time* – Practise sudden jumps backwards, from the last stance.

Teaching point
A quick take-off will be achieved if the body is tensed first in preparation.

Exploring the route into the tomb is the final section and will be improvised.

Making the dance

① Repeat your strolling, stopping to contemplate for a set number of times (three or four). Then spring back as though leaping back into history and the journey into the tomb begins . . . .

② The route into the tombs was often twisting, narrow and maze-like, to deter thieves. Imagine you are moving in the dark along an unknown passage, tentatively exploring your way with hands and feet as you move slowly into the unknown . . . .

Contemplating

Teaching point
*Using the imagination will conjure up images
of smooth walls, rough ground, narrow gaps to
be squeezed through, ascending or descending.*

③ Invent an ending according to what you
see as you emerge into the tomb. Find a
way of reacting to it, ending with a still
position.

Teaching point
*Pupils try to make it clear from their reaction
how they feel about what they have seen.*

Sharing the work

Half-class demonstrations.

Teaching points
*(a) Comment upon the still positions that
capture the atmosphere of viewing in a
museum.*
*(b) Which dancers have used good imagination
in the passages section?*

Possible developments

Plan the next section of the dance to the
title: 'The Pharaoh's Revenge'.

The teacher's own notes

4.5   The Pyramids

The dance looks at Ancient Egypt's most famous monuments, the pyramids, which were built by hand without modern-day technology – an amazing feat.

Resources

1. Pictures of the pyramids, or of the methods used in the building.

2. Music: 'Samba Tachycardia'. *Drummin' 'n Dancin'*. Primrose Educational Resources.

Exploring the ideas

Building

☐1 Describe ways in which the huge blocks of stone which make up the pyramids were moved, by hand.

Teaching point
Select words which particularly represent the effort involved, e.g. heaving, hauling, levering, dragging, bearing, etc.

☐2 Explore on your own ideas for showing these actions.

Teaching points
(a) Encourage a low, stable stance. Are the steps large or small? Would you move fast or slow? What grip are you using?

(b) There should be a rhythm to the energy factor, where the power is gathered in the preparation, applied in the action phase and released during the recovery.

☐3 In fours, find ways of transporting in which you have to work co-operatively to show the amount of effort or force required.

Teaching point
Keeping a rhythmic movement will keep the group to work together.

The pyramid is finished

In fours, find ways of working in contact to make a group design to represent the pyramid itself. Try several alternatives. Plan how you will move in and out of the design. Choose your most original idea and practise it until you can perform it well and hold it as this will be your finishing position for the dance.

Teaching point
Emphasise that a wide, stable base and taking each other's weight, if appropriate, may help to create the sloping sides of the pyramid.

Making the dance

In groups of four, perform your transporting action a set number of times and then finish by moving into and holding your pyramid shape.

Teaching point
The number of repetitions will depend on the length of the transporting actions and is decided by the teacher.

The pyramids

40

Sharing the work

Two or three teams demonstrate at once.

Teaching points
(a) The observers should look for groups which look as though they are moving massive weights, by their use of dynamics, body position, etc.

(b) The most inventive solutions to the pyramid design should be noted.

Possible developments

◇1 The teacher arranges groups, so that the working actions are performed as a chain reaction.

◇2 Groups could be larger which will make more solutions possible in the pyramid section.

◇3 Repeat the working action and finish with a whole-class pyramid.

The teacher's own notes

Theme 5   Dance by Chance

This theme introduces the ideas that dance can be made up through random choice, a technique sometimes used by choreographers such as Merce Cunningham. It can serve to introduce pupils to the concepts of movements, dynamics, directions etc. and also help them to begin to explore ways of structuring their dances for themselves.

5.1   My Word!

This introduces pupils to a way of using vocabulary as a means of determining the action, dynamics, possibly the flow and spatial elements. Given these elements, interpretation into movement and the choice of order are preliminary stages of choreography.

Resources

Word list, either given example or one devised by teacher, printed onto different coloured paper:

● *Travel* – Run Walk Shuffle Prowl Skip Gallop Rush Slide Dart Skim Crawl Creep Stride Drag Whiz Retreat Whoosh Tip-toe Plod Zoom.

● *Jump* – Explode Soar Gallop Skip Launch Leap Bounce Spring Pop Bubble Fly Hop.

● *Turn* – Spin Roll Swirl Coil Rotate Spiral Whirl Whip Wind.

● *Gesture* – Stretch Curl Expand Contract Extend Swell Reach Lean Squeeze Shake Scatter Flop Enclose Pull Crumple Collapse Jerk Quiver Push Clap Tap Twist Pierce Gather Shrink Wrap Tip Twine Wring Entangle.

● *Stopping* – Freeze Hover Settle Pause Hesitate Brake Complete Halt.

● *Extra pile for development work* – Recoil Shatter Fragment Cascade Splinter Reflect Cling Project Fold Rebound Envelop Grip Lock Escape Compress.

Recoil

42

Exploring the ideas

1 Select a slip containing one word from each of five different coloured piles. Each colour specifies a particular type of movement, i.e. gesture, turn, travel, jump, stopping.

Teaching point
Pupils may need help with some words, depending on their age and ability.

2 Now experiment with ways of interpreting each word in dance, by trying out a variety of alternatives. Then select one movement for each word from your own ideas.

Teaching points
(a) It is essential that pupils are encouraged and given time to explore possibilities.

(b) The word contains clues to the dynamics (i.e. the qualitative elements such as 'powerfully', 'lightly', 'swiftly', 'slowly', 'continuously' or 'intermittently' etc.) and pupils should be guided to show these clearly.

Making the dance

Decide on the order of the five words chosen, plan the links between the actions and practise them to make a whole dance.

Teaching point
The comparison with writing a coherent sentence – i.e. a logical order, fluent style, well expressed, etc. – will help pupils to understand some of the elements of composition.

Sharing the work

All pupils perform their solos in groups.

Teaching point
Observers look for dances which are fluent and attention catching, and then explain, with examples, their choices of good work.

Possible developments

◇ A sixth pile of words which are more demanding (see list) which will be assigned to pupils who are coping easily with the original task and need extending.

◇ Partner work. Consider how the two original 'dance sentences' can be made to interact as a duo, i.e. by considering how they share the space, whether there are common time elements, etc.

◇ Pupils are set the follow-up task of finding one unusual word for each category before the following lesson.

The teacher's own notes

5.2 Three Card Hand

Here the cards determine the action and speed of movement. Pupils then have the opportunity to make choices about how to construct these into the dance. Knowledge of the range of alternatives given in the vocabularly from Unit 5.1 (*My Word!*, page 42) will enrich their options.

Resources

Three packs of playing cards, excluding jokers.

Exploring the ideas

Pupils are each dealt three cards. The suit determines the action (e.g. clubs = turning; diamonds = travelling; hearts = jumping; and spades = gesturing). Whether the number is odd or even determines the energy dynamic (e.g. odd numbers means performed with strong tension, even numbers with light tension). Picture cards give free choice of dynamics.

Explore a variety of ways of translating each action into dance and from this select one for each card.

Teaching points
(a) Allow time for and encourage the exploration stage, as this will determine the quality and originality of the finished dances.
(b) Recalling the options from My Word unit may be helpful.
(c) Pupils may naturally associate powerful movements with speed and light tension movements with slowness. The alternatives should be encouraged, as should gradual as well as abrupt transitions of dynamics. If necessary, revise the use of dynamics by giving pupils appropriate tasks.

Making the dance

Choose the order, combine the elements and practise until the dance becomes a whole.

Teaching point
Observe and comment on the way in which the energy dynamic is being developed.

Jumping explosively

44

Sharing the work

Work in twos, one performing, one observing, to check whether the dance contains the three prescribed actions. Then each partner observes a second time to see how the dynamics are being used.

Teaching point
Observers should give sensitive and constructive feedback, the dancer then performs again and the observer looks for improvement.

Possible developments

◇1 The odd/even can be used to determine different pairs of dynamics, e.g. fast/slow or the flow factor (free flowing or more contained).

◇2 Picture cards can be used to designate level (others have free choice) e.g. Jack has to be performed at low level, Queen at medium and King at high level.

◇3 Pupils may use more than three cards.

◇4 Jokers give complete free choice of action and dynamic.

The teacher's own notes

5.3 Chance Encounters

Pupils develop individual dance from a movement-based task. The unit emphasises the way in which moments of interaction between dancers can raise through happy accident rather than planning. It develops awareness of the need to observe for and capitalise on these.

Resources

1. Videoing the work will enable participants to see it and also observers to review it and possibly evaluate how many of the encounters they noticed.

2. Music: Cello Concerto in D Minor. Vivaldi or Bodinerie Bach. Both tracks appear on *Editions de l'Oiseau-Lyre*. Decca.

Exploring the ideas

Take the four words: **launch — slide — expanding** — squeeze working by yourself, interpret them into movement and perform them in this order. The first stage is to experiment with alternative ways of taking each word into dance.

Making the dance

Select, link together and practise the dance phrase.

Teaching point
Dancers will need to remember their dances accurately for the next stage.

Sharing the work

This is the major part of the lesson as the intention is to develop the observation skills and make pupils aware that a chance element can introduce interesting interaction, and as choreographers they need to be alert to this.

Everyone will perform in groups of five, each having been given a number, 1 to 5. Start, stop or continue your movement phrase when your number is called out (by the teacher in the first instance). Perform your phrase over and over again, until the demonstration ends.

Teaching points
(a) Performers start relatively near to the others and stay aware of other dancers, so that some 'chance encounters' are more likely to happen. Each must be completely still when asked to stop and also remember the dance to re-commence.

(b) The teacher uses the option of calling numbers to elicit as many interactions as possible.

(c) Observers note and comment on the 'chance encounters' which they see and describe their response to these.

Slide

Possible developments

◇1 Vary the words for the dance phrase.

◇2 Instead of pupils deciding a dance phrase, a phrase taught by the teacher is used which all the dancers learn.

◇3 Pupils observing can call the numbers.

◇4 Dancers can call the numbers.

◇5 Teacher determines which front each performer will start facing.

The teacher's own notes

5.4 Where to Now?

Here the only element of the dance which is prescribed is the place in the performing area to which pupils must move. Choice of movements is left to the individual dancer.

Resources

1. Prepared numbered sheets to identify squares in the grid.

2. Several dice. If two colours are not available, pupils are designated 'blue' or 'red' before they throw.

3. Pencils and paper for pupils to record their routes.

Making the dance

The movement phrase should be performed, starting within the first square, along the plotted pathway and finishing in the last numbered square given.

Exploring the ideas

The floor is divided into a grid of 12 areas, numbered 1 to 6 in red and 1 to 6 in blue. The centre of each is marked with a numbered, colour-coded piece of paper taped to the floor.

1 Make six throws of a red **or** blue dice and record your six numbers in the order thrown. This order, representing squares on the grid, gives you the route you must travel along in the dance.

2 Revise a dance phrase learnt in any previous lesson **or** make one up using four words from the list given in Unit 5.1 (*My Word*, page 42).

Teaching point
Each pupil needs to walk their route and make sure that they know the order of the references on the floor grid.

Crumple

48

Teaching points

(a) It may be necessary to repeat the phrase more than once to reach the end of the route.

(b) The pathways between each square may be curved, zig-zag etc. rather than on a direct line each time.

(c) Ask pupils to consider which movements offer a choice of travelling or on the spot (e.g. turning) and use these to give variety.

Sharing the work

Half-class demonstrations

Teaching points

(a) Observers look for the effects of how using different pathways can enhance the effect of the movement.

(b) Observers should be able to comment on the effect of distance from the audience of the impact made by a movement.

Possible developments

◇ Relating or reversing the route. Making changes of direction whilst on the route.

◇ Combine this idea with that in *Chance Encounters* (page 46), so that as dancers follow their own routes they also take opportunities for interaction.

5.5 Consequences

This dance explores possibilities which arise when pupils determine the actions, dynamics and leading parts of the body, but the combination is random.

Resources

Pencil and paper, one per pupil.

Exploring the ideas

☐1 Class discussion on the way in which 'Consequences' is played, and the need to set realistic challenges!

☐2 In threes, each of you writes a part of the body on the top of your sheet of paper and folds it over before handing it on. Without reading what was previously written, then write an action on this sheet and again fold it and hand it on. The third time, write an adverb, i.e. a word which describes **how** the movement is to be done, e.g. explosively, sadly, reluctantly etc.

The process is repeated three times in all and then pass on your papers for the last time, open them and read the instructions. At this stage you realise the importance of giving practicable and imaginative suggestions!

☐3 Experiment with ways of carrying out each action with the body part indicated and in the way stated, for instance, 'shoulder' 'rises' 'agitatedly'.

Teaching points
(a) Some of the resulting combinations may be humorous or even seemingly contradictory, but the intention is to stimulate imaginative ideas and creative interpretations, so these should be encouraged.

(b) Although only one part of the body is designated, the whole body should be involved and used imaginatively, e.g. inverting.

Making the dance

The three given actions are now combined, in any order, to form a dance phrase.

Teaching points
(a) Experimenting with the order will help to establish which is the best.

(b) Encourage originality, rather than a quick, problem-solving approach.

Piercing slowly with the elbow

Sharing the work

① In threes, each perform to the other two, who can then see how the ideas they contributed have been applied.

Teaching point
The criteria for comment is how imaginative, rather than how accurate, the interpretation has been.

② Each trio then decides through discussion which of the three dances is the most original, and the nominated pupils then perform to the remainder of the class.

Possible developments

◇ The nine ideas could be developed into a trio dance.

◇ Linking actions could be added between the prescribed movements to extend the dance.

The teacher's own notes

Theme 6 **Language**

6.1 Partner Work through Words

Ideas for contact work in duos are introduced.

Resources

1. Dictionary and thesaurus.

2. Videos of professional dance pieces involving contact work.

3. Music: 'He Ain't Heavy, He's my Brother'. *20 Golden Greats*. The Hollies. EMI TCATAK 38.

Exploring the ideas

☐1 Taking some or all of these words:
lean — lift — carry — balance — propel.
Explore possible interpretations in pairs.

Teaching points
(a) SAFETY: Stress to pupils that partner's safety is very important and attempt only activities which are within their skills level.

(b) Organising children into pairs of roughly the same height will make it more likely that both partners will have a turn at both roles.

(c) Trying to find more variations, where both partners are reliant on the other for **lean** *and* **balance,** *as well as those where one partner is dominant will extend the work.*

☐2 Agree and select the ideas you want to use in the dance.

Making the dance

Experiment with ways of combining or linking the movements you have chosen. Try different possibilities until you have a phrase that is fluent and which you can perform well.

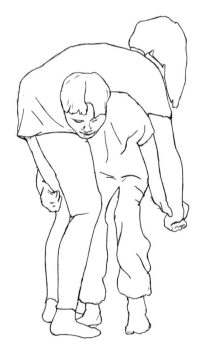

Lifting

52

Teaching points
(a) Encourage pupils to work at different speeds, whilst maintaining control.
*(b) Timing will be very important in the **lift** and **propel** parts, where the partner's momentum may be used.*

Sharing the work

Quarter-class demonstrations.

Teaching points
(a) Imaginative, rather than functional interpretations of the task should be noted.
(b) High levels of co-operative working should also be praised.

Possible developments

① Trio work.
② Adding other words which use partner work, suggested by pupils.

The teacher's own notes

6.2 Poetry

A poem acts as the stimulus for the dance; a selection of lines, phrases or words is made and translated into the medium of movement.

The poem used is called 'Mindgames' and was written by a 14 year old in response to the idea of taking a journey inside one's own head. It is not necessary when taking a poem as a stimulus to interpret the whole or even complete lines, fragments and odd words may spark off ideas for dance.

Resources

1. Poem. Mindgames. *See* page 55.

2. Music: Suspense'. *Music and Image Teaching Pack.* Museum of Moving Image Education Department.

Exploring the ideas

1 Look at copies of the poem and discuss with a partner the lines which appeal to you as the basis for a dance.

2 Experiment with ways of using the chosen extract(s), ranging from a single phrase to a line or section of the poem.

Teaching points
(a) Allow time to try several ideas and select the ones which generate the best dance ideas.

(b) Pupils should try to capture the essence of the extract, by developing a response which goes beyond the mimetic, for example, through enlarging the movement and repeating it.

(c) Encourage pupils to use the phrase to free the imagination rather than limit the response.

(d) Some of the experience from Unit 6.1 (Partner Work Through Words, page 52) may prove helpful.

3 Select in consultation the ideas which you intend to use in the final dance.

Making the dance

This dance, in particular, needs a clear beginning and end and to include a climax, because of the dramatic nature of the poem. With this in mind, plan the order of your ideas. Practise and refine them into a short dance.

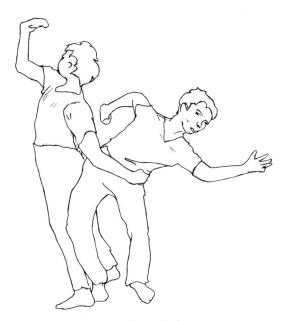

'Sticking to the lanes of wonder'

Teaching point
Suggest to pupils that they will need to
consider how the dance develops the
relationship within the duo; for example, are
the two working together? In opposition? In
isolation? The use or absence of contact, the
distance between the orientation of the dancers
will help to determine this.

Sharing the work

Half the class demonstrates, in pairs.

Teaching point
Keeping the poem in mind, observers select the
pairs they think have captured the poem in
their dances.

Possible developments

◇ Assign different lines or parts of the
poem to different pairs/groups. The
performance can be of short phrases and
be performed consecutively.

◇ A group dance can be developed if the
teacher chooses an order, so that pairs
perform more than one at a time, with
overlap, each pair entering and leaving the
performance space in turn.

Mindgames

Calling the horrors around the corner
Climbing the steps of panic
Stroking the chamber of terror
Dancing in and out of fantasy
Exploring the caves of secrecy
Passing through the winding passages of hatred
Pressing the pain of jealousy
Clawing the corridors of sorrow
Pulling the strings of gaiety
Crossing the bridge of guilt
Echoing the whisper of doubt
Patting the alleyways of annoyance
Sticking to the lanes of wonder
Scratching out the memories
Dragging up the memories
Shouting out the guilt
Jumping the ditches of confusion
Falling down the well of demands
Swallowed up by unhappiness

The teacher's own notes

6.3 Headlines

The headline or title gives a brief insight into what is to come. Here it acts as a stimulus to the creation of a dance.

Resources

A variety of newspaper headlines.

Exploring the ideas

Pupils look at and select from a limited choice of headlines (from newspapers or magazines), choosing them for the dance potential which they see in it. The teacher needs to have selected titles which will capture the imagination of the class and also have implicit movement potential. They can be simple or more complex depending on the experience and skills of the class. For example, **Chaos!'** may be more straightforward, whereas **'Will this never end?** may be more ambiguous and therefore sets a more open-ended task.

1 Consider your chosen headline and decide which dynamics will be appropriate according to the interpretation you choose to put on it.

Teaching points
(a) The options for dynamics will include:
Variations of speed – i.e. hustling, dragging, hestitating, etc.
Variations of tension/energy – i.e. floppily, forcefully, delicately.

(b) The choice may include a contrast or range of dynamics.

2 Establish a motif or movement phrase (i.e. short movement or few movements linked) for the headline.

Teaching point
The essential point is that the dynamics chosen are incorporated as these will remain constant.

3 The motif should then be performed using the following variations:

● Reverse the motif.
● Develop the motif into travelling or perform on the spot.
● Change the level at which the motif is performed.

This gives four versions from which the dance will be made.

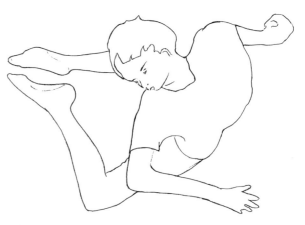

'Chaos!'

56

Making the dance

Take the four chosen ideas and combine them.

Teaching points
(a) Remind pupils that the dynamics remain constant.

It will be important to stress that the linking of the variations needs to be planned.

Sharing the work

All pupils perform their solos, several at a time.

Teaching point
(a) Observers should look for dances where the development of the original motif is clear.

Selected pupils are asked to say their headlines and explain their interpretations before performing.

Possible developments

Rather than keep the dynamics constant, other factors are chosen; for example, the spatial elements. The variations are then developed around others aspects, for example the speed at which the motif is performed could change.

The teacher's own notes

6.4 Narrative

The outline of the story is told through dance.

Resources

1. The text of *Macbeth* by William Shakespeare.

2. *Tales from Shakespeare* by Charles and Mary Lamb.

3. Pictures of the characters.

4. Copies of the quotations.

5. Music: 'Dance of the Knights'. *Romeo and Juliet*. Prokoviev. Many versions.

Exploring the ideas

There is a choice of three scenes, taken from the story of *Macbeth:* the meeting of the witches on the heath, Macbeth's vision of the dagger and Lady Macbeth's repeated efforts to wash the blood from her hands.

1 *The meeting of the witches*
'Double, double, toil and trouble; fire burn and cauldron bubble . . . Eye of newt and toe of frog, wool of bat and tongue of dog'.
Macbeth. IV.I.

In groups of three, explore body shapes, gestures and ways of travelling round together which show distortion.

Teaching point
Encourage angular shapes, asymmetry and using joints to lead the movements.

2 *The vision of the dagger.*
'Is this a dagger which I see before me? The handle towards my hand? Come let me clutch thee . . . a dagger of the mind, a false creation'.

Macbeth. II.I

Explore the ideas of seeing visions. From a still position, focus on a distant point, show a way of reacting to the imaginary dagger, i.e. recoiling, being drawn, looking away. Develop ways of reaching for it, hesitating as you do so, or snatching at it, only to find that the vision is not real and reappears elsewhere in the room.

Teaching point
In order to capture the drama of the scene pupils should be encouraged to avoid straightforward mimetic interpretations, by involving the whole body in the actions.

'Out damned spot!'

③ *Washing the hands.*
'Out, damned spot! Out I say! . . . What!
Will these hands ne'er be clean? . . . All
the perfumes of Arabia will not sweeten
this little hand'.

Macbeth. V.1.

Taking the gesture of washing the hands,
increase the power and energy with which
this is done to express Lady's Macbeth's
frantic feelings. Now repeat this, as though
the whole body were the hands, i.e.
twisting, wringing and wiping actions.

Teaching point
*The motif can be built up from the single
gesture of washing the hands to the whole-
body one, which will create a natural
progression.*

Making the dance

Whichever scene is chosen, select from the
ideas developed in the exploratory section
and make them into a short dance phrase.
The phrase may be repeated to a climax,
to emphasise the dramatic nature of the
play.

Teaching point
*The drama will be expressed through the
dynamics and the use of focus. These will
therefore need to be carefully planned and
performed.*

Sharing the work

All the work is performed in groups.

Teaching point
*Observers look for and comment on the
dramatic intensity of the performance and
discuss how this is achieved.*

Possible developments

① More than one scene could be chosen
and the dances linked.

② Pupils who have studied the play could
suggest further scenes.

③ The three scenes could be performed
simultaneously by a group of three (the
witches) and two solo dancers representing
Macbeth's vision and Lady Macbeth's
hand-washing. The dance making would
involve ways of co-ordinating these.

The teacher's own notes

59

6.5 The Spoken Word

Resources

1. Copies of the text. *See* page 62.
2. A spoken recording of the speech.
3. Information about the American Civil Rights movement, in the 1960s.

Exploring the ideas

The text used in Martin Luther King's 'I have a dream . . .'

The words of the text are used as stimulus for the dance as in the Unit 6.2 (*Poetry*, page 54) but here the spoken word is used as an accompaniment. This provides a setting and an atmosphere for the dance, determining the dynamics, the phrasing and the length of the whole dance.

The text is used to help to structure a whole-class dance. Pairs of pupils are asked to use either the odd- or even-numbered lines.

1 The first stages of the exploration are the same as for Unit 6.2 (page 54).

2 Experiment with ways of interpreting your given lines through dance, so that the dance phrase lasts as long as the spoken line and finishes with a moment of stillness which can be held.

Teaching point
The message of the whole speech should be shown through the interaction of the two dancers. Because each line is relatively short, the ideas will have to be concentrated, possible at times into a single gesture.

Making the dance

The lines will be linked through held positions (whilst the other half of the class performs the alternate line).

Teaching point
Pupils may need to be reminded that the finishing position for each line will need to be the starting point for the next.

Sharing the work

Half of the 'even-line' pairs and half of the 'odd-line' pairs perform at the same time, whilst the lines are being spoken. Remainder observe.

Teaching point
Observers look for and notice pairs who have concentrated the meaning of the line into their dance.

'With this faith we will be able to work together'

Possible developments

◇1 Pupils could take other speeches or spoken texts from which to work.

◇2 Use of song; the lyrics can be used in the same way as the spoken text.

◇3 Conversation as the stimulus for the dance.

The teacher's own notes

I HAVE A DREAM . . .

I say to you today, even though we face the difficulties of today and tomorrow, I still have a dream.

It is a dream that is deeply rooted in the American dream.
I have a dream that one day this nation will rise up, live out the true meaning of its creed.

We hold these truths to be self-evident that all men are created equal.
I have a dream that one day on the red hills of Georgia, the sons of former slaves and the sons of former slave-owners will be able to sit down together at the table of brotherhood.

I have a dream that one day, even in the state of Mississippi, a state sweltering with the heat of oppression will be transformed into an oasis of freedom and justice.

I have a dream that my four little children will one day live in a nation where they will not be judged by the colour of their skin, but by the content of their character.

I have a dream that one day every valley shall be exalted, every hill and mountain shall be made low. The rough places will be made plain and the crooked places will be made straight.

This is the faith that I go back to the south with.
With this faith, we will be able to hew out of the mountains of despair, the stone of hope.

With this faith we will be able to work together, to pray together, to struggle together, to go to jail together, to stand up for freedom together, knowing we will be free one day.

This will be the day that all of God's children will be able to sing with new meaning 'Let freedom ring!'

So let freedom ring from the prodigious hilltops of New Hampshire,
let freedom ring from the mighty mountains of New York, but not only that let freedom ring from stone mountain of Georgia. Let freedom ring from every hill and molehill of Mississippi, from every mountainside.

When we allow freedom to ring from every town and every hamlet from every state and every city, we will be able to speed up that day when all of God's children, black men and white men, Jews and Gentiles, Protestants and Catholics will be able to join hands and sing in the words of the old negro spiritual:

'Free at last! Free at last! Great God almighty! We are free at last!

Martin Luther King.